COLLINS YOUNG CLASSICS

THE SECRET GARDEN

Abridged by Joyce McAleer
from the story by Frances Hodgson Burnett
Illustrated by Alison Nicholson

A NEW HOME

When Mary Lennox first came to England, people said what a sickly and sad child she seemed. She was so thin, with wispy hair and a bad-tempered look on her face all the time.

It was no wonder that poor Mary looked so ill and unhappy. She had lived in India with her mother and her father, who had an important job. One terrible day, she woke up to find her parents, the servants and nearly everyone else around had died from a dreadful disease called cholera. Mary was all alone, so she was sent to live with her hunchback uncle in Misselthwaite Manor, a large old house, on the Yorkshire Moors.

At first, Mary thought her new home very strange. The people spoke in a funny way, and it was cold, with howling winds and rain lashing over the wild moor. There were a hundred rooms, though most of them were shut up. Mary's uncle, Mr Archibald Craven, did not wish to meet her when she arrived.

"He won't see people," said Mrs Medlock, the housekeeper. "Since his wife died, he's been so unhappy, he shuts himself up in the West Wing."

Mary soon got to know the other servants, especially Martha, the maid. In India, Mary had been used to telling servants exactly what to do, and they always obeyed; here, they were friendly and said

whatever they liked. In India everything had been done for her; now she had to learn to do things for herself.

At first, this made her angry, but as time passed, she became less like the spoiled, spiteful little girl she had been.

Martha talked a lot in her funny Yorkshire way. She babbled on about her family who lived in a little cottage. She told Mary about her young brother, Dickon, who played on the moor for hours and hours, all by himself. He was friends with the animals and birds.

One wintry day, as Mary went out to play, Martha said a curious thing, "One of th' gardens is locked up. No one has been in it for ten years. Mr Craven had it shut when his wife died so sudden. He won't let no-one go inside. It was her garden. He locked th' door an' dug a hole and buried the key."

Mary was thinking how strange it was, when she met old Ben, the gardener. Mary told him how lonely she felt, and Ben replied that *his* only friend was a little robin. When he whistled, the robin flew to him and sang. Mary loved to see this, and she made friends with the robin, too.

Every day, Mary played by herself. She wandered around the kitchen garden and the orchard and watched Ben working. The cold wind almost took her breath away as it swept down from the moor, so Mary ran to keep warm. The fresh air was good for her. She

began to eat more, and stopped turning up her nose at her porridge each morning. Her face stopped being a sickly yellow colour and her eyes sparkled a little. She was really beginning to like being out of doors, whatever the weather. Martha had told her mother all about Mary's lonely life. Feeling sorry for her, the kindly old lady had given her a skipping rope. Mary was delighted with it and played with it everyday.

Mary longed to see inside the hidden garden. She was sure which one it was: the one at the end of the orchard. The walls were so covered with ivy that the door could not be seen. Martha said her uncle's wife had fallen from a branch in the garden and then died. That was why he hated it so.

Sometimes it rained for days, and the wind howled and howled. It was cosy sitting in her room, gazing into the roaring fire and listening to Martha's chatter.

It was on a day like this, with a gale blowing around the huge house, that Mary heard a very disturbing sound. At first she thought it was the wind, but the more she listened, the more she was sure it was the sound of a child crying, somewhere inside the house.

"Do you hear anyone crying?" she asked Martha.

"It's th' wind . . . it makes all sorts o' sounds."

But Mary knew it wasn't the wind – and she could tell that Martha knew too.

A couple of days later, the dreadful storm was over, and the sky was a brilliant, deep blue. Mary went outside and met old Ben.

"Springtime's comin', " he said. "Can th' smell it?"

Mary sniffed; everything smelt new and fresh and damp. It gave her a good feeling. She asked Ben about the flowers that would come in Spring.

"Crocus an' snowdrops an' daffydowndillys," said Ben. "Has th' never seen them?"

"No. Everything is hot and wet and green in India after the rain." She could hardly wait to see what an English springtime was like.

Mary wandered away from Ben, the same way she always went, towards what she thought was the secret garden. She gazed at the walls, so densely covered with ivy, with trees peeping out over the top.

MARY FINDS A KEY

Suddenly the most exciting thing happened! She heard a chirp and twitter – and there was a robin. He had followed her.

"You remember me!" cried Mary.

The robin chirped away, just as if he were talking. Then he began to dig in the ground, as if for worms, but he kept on digging, quite deep. Mary looked, and blinked – and looked again. What was that? The robin had unearthed something. She trembled a little as she picked up a rusty old metal object. Mary gasped with delight – it was a key!

She held the key for a long time. Could it be to the secret garden? She put it in her pocket and vowed to keep it there, until she found the hidden door.

The next day Mary took her rope and skipped around the gardens, down her favourite walk – the one that led to the hidden garden. When she had first arrived at Misselthwaite she could hardly skip at all, but now she could skip longer and longer every day.

She saw the robin near the wall. "You showed me where the key was. Now show me the door."

Afterwards, Mary always said that what happened next was magic – and who knows? Maybe it was!

The little robin flew onto a branch of ivy and sang a lovely song. Then a gust of wind blew aside some of the trailing ivy – and there, right before her eyes, was the knob of a door!

Mary put the key in the lock. It was stiff – but it did turn. Very slowly she pushed open the door. Shaking and breathing fast with excitement, she entered the secret garden!

It was an enchanting and mysterious place, with everything overgrown. Thick, climbing roses covered the high walls, and some had tendrils which swung down over other trees like swaying curtains.

"How still it is," whispered Mary, "and no wonder. I am the first person who has spoken in here for ten years."

The robin was still too. He sat on his tree-top without stirring. Mary hoped the garden was alive. Then she noticed some pale green points sticking out from the earth; growing things!

Although she knew nothing about gardening, Mary found a sharp stick and cleared away the weeds from around the little plants so that they could breathe. She did this all around the secret garden, and enjoyed herself so much and grew so warm she had to take her coat off!

Mary skipped home happily. She had such red cheeks and such bright eyes and ate such a dinner that Martha was delighted.

"Eh! My mother will be pleased when I tell her what th' skippin' rope's done for thee!" said Martha.

"I wish I had a little spade too," said Mary.

Martha thought this was a good idea. She had no idea that Mary had found the secret garden, of course. "Th' shop in th' village sells little garden sets: a spade, rake an' fork all for two shillings. They sell seeds, too."

"I've got enough money," said Mary eagerly.

"My brother Dickon will get them for you!" Martha wrote a note to Dickon, and put it in an envelope with the money. "The butcher's boy will take it to him," she said.

Mary thought how wonderful it would be to meet Dickon.

All through the following week Mary visited her secret garden. She loved being shut in behind its beautiful old walls. It was like a fairy-tale place.

Mary tried to find out about flowers and plants from Ben, but she had to be careful not to give away her secret. Ben told her he liked roses best of all, because he used to work for a lady who had roses in a special place she loved.

"That was about ten years ago," said Ben.

"Where is she now?" asked Mary.

"Heaven," answered Ben.

"What happened to the roses?"

"Once or twice a year I'd go an' prune 'em a bit."

"Don't you go now?" Mary felt quite excited. Ben was obviously talking about the roses in the secret garden!

"Not this year. I've been too stiff in th' joints." Suddenly, Ben became quite angry. "Don't ask so many questions," he scowled.

DICKON!

After this, Mary skipped off down to the walk which curved round the secret garden. It ended in a gate leading to a wood. A low, whistling sound came from beyond the gate. Mary went through and saw a boy sitting under a tree and playing on a wooden pipe. He was about twelve, with a turned-up nose, red cheeks and the bluest eyes Mary had ever seen. As he stopped playing, a squirrel scampered back to a tree and rabbits hopped away.

"I'm Dickon," he said. "And you're Miss Mary. I've brought your garden tools and seeds."

Mary was so pleased! She and Dickon sat down on a log and he showed her the little packets of seeds, each with a picture of a flower. Suddenly, he asked, "Where's that robin as is callin' us?"

"Is he really calling us?" said Mary.

"Aye. He's callin' someone he's friends with."

Mary told him about Ben's robin. "I think he knows me, too."

"Aye, he'll tell me all about thee, later."

Dickon could understand birds and animals. "Sometimes I think I'm one of 'em," he said, "a bird, or a fox or rabbit or squirrel. I've lived on th' moor with them for so long."

Mary listened in wonder.

Then Dickon said, "I'll plant the seeds for thee. Where's tha' garden?"

Poor Mary's face turned red. "Can you keep a secret?" she asked.

Dickon smiled, "I keep secrets from the other lads about nests an' other wild things, or there'd be naught safe on th' moor."

Mary spurted out, "I've stolen a garden. Nobody wants it, nobody cares for it . . . but I want it to be alive. I'll show you."

Dickon stood in the secret garden and whispered, "I never thought I'd see this place."

"You knew about it?"

Dickon nodded. "Martha told me. I used to wonder what it was like."

Mary eagerly showed Dickon round.

"Who did that?" he cried, pointing to where she had cleared the ground around the green points.

"I did," said Mary.

Dickon told her she had done very well. "A gardener couldn't have done better!"

As he examined the roses, he seemed puzzled. "There's been a bit o' prunin' done here. Someone besides the robin has been here since ten years ago."

Mary was so happy she had shared the secret. "Promise you'll never tell," she said.

Dickon grinned, "If tha' were a missel thrush an' tha' showed me thy nest, I'd wouldn't tell. Your secret's that safe!"

MARY MEETS HER UNCLE

Mary's uncle spent most of the time away, but now he was back and he asked to meet Mary. At once Mary noticed how unhappy he seemed. His shoulders were a bit crooked, but he would have been quite handsome if he had not been so sad.

"I know nothing about children," he said. "Is there anything you need?"

"Might I have a bit of earth," asked Mary, "to grow things in?"

"You can have as much earth as you want," said her uncle. "You remind me of someone who loved gardens. When you see a bit of earth you want, take it."

"Might I take it from anywhere – if it's not wanted?"

"Anywhere!"

It rained that night, and the wind howled. Mary lay in bed, listening. And then she heard that crying sound again.

"I will find out what it is," she said to herself.

So, taking a candle, she tiptoed softly down the

long, dark corridor to where the noise was coming from. Finally, she stood outside a room, her heart beating fast. This was it!

Mary entered the room. It was very large and, lying on a bed, was a boy with a thin pale face and huge eyes. As Mary approached him, he whispered, "Are you a ghost?"

"No, are you?"

"No, I am Colin Craven. Who are you?"

"Mary Lennox. Mr Craven is my uncle."

"He is my father."

They were both amazed, because neither knew the other existed.

"I am always ill and have to stay here," said Colin. "If I live, I will have a crooked back like my father's. He can hardly bear to look at me, because my mother died when I was born."

Mary and Colin talked for a long time.

"How old are you?" he asked her.

"I am ten," said Mary, "and so are you. I know that because when you were born, the garden was locked up and the key buried."

This interested and excited Colin. He made Mary tell him about the secret garden. She told him as much as she could without actually admitting that she had found it.

"I want to see that garden!" declared Colin.

Then he told Mary to pull aside a curtain which was hanging over a picture on the wall. The laughing girl in the picture had dark eyes like Colin's.

"That is my mother," said the boy. "If she hadn't died, my father wouldn't be so unhappy, and I might not be so ill."

TEMPERS AND MAGIC

Next day Mary startled Martha by saying, "I found out what the crying was. It was Colin. I met him."

"I'll be in trouble!"

"No, you won't."

"But he won't let strangers look at him."

"He *let me*, and he showed me his mother's picture. I think he almost liked me. He's a very spoilt boy."

Martha could hardly believe this. "Tha' must have bewitched him," she gasped.

"You mean magic? I've heard about magic, but I can't make it. I just went into his room and we talked and talked. He didn't want me to leave. What exactly is the matter with him?"

"Nobody knows for sure. When he was born the master wouldn't set eyes on him. He said he'd have a crooked back, just like his own."

"Has Colin got a crooked back?"

"Once they made him wear a brace, but another doctor came from London an' made them take it off. Oh, he's had lots o' illness but he has a terrible temper and always gets his own way."

Later that day, Colin sent for Mary. She told him about Dickon and how he could charm the animals and birds. Colin was fascinated. "I could never go out on the moor," he grumbled.

"You might – some time."

"But I'm ill. Everybody wishes I'd die."

Mary had no patience with this. It made her feel very contrary indeed. "If everybody wished that I would die – then I simply wouldn't!" she declared firmly.

It rained for another week, and Mary visited Colin every day. They talked about all kinds of things, and they even laughed! Colin wanted to hear about India and gardens and Dickon. They looked at books and pictures. Colin seemed much happier.

"It's been a blessing," said Mrs Medlock! "He's not had a tantrum since he made friends with you!"

One morning Mary awoke to find the sun shining into her room. The sky was a glorious blue and the whole world looked as if magic had been worked on it. A great waft of warm, fresh, scented air blew in, and birds sang with the joy of spring.

Mary dressed quickly and ran down to the secret garden. Dickon was there, working. A rook landed on his shoulder and a little fox cub scrambled along by his side. Ben's robin flew by, busily building its nest. Everything was bursting with life!

"I'm so happy!" cried Mary.

As they both worked in the garden, Mary told Dickon about Colin. Dickon was relieved, because he knew about him already. He had heard Mrs. Medlock telling his mother.

"He needs fresh air," said Mary. "I wonder if he could keep a secret and let us bring him here. You could push his carriage."

"It'd do him good," replied Dickon. "We'd be just three children watchin' a garden grow. It'd be better than medicine for th' lad!"

Mary was too busy in the garden to visit Colin that morning. Martha told her that this had upset him, but Mary had no sympathy. She forgot what a spoilt girl she had been when she lived in India and how she used to behave like Colin herself.

When Mary did go to see Colin, she found him lying in bed in a miserable state.

"Why didn't you come to see me?" he whined.

"I was in the garden, with Dickon."

"I'll send that common boy away if you play with him instead of me!"

Mary flew into a rage, "If you do. I'll never come to see you again!"

"You will if I say so!" stormed Colin.

"I won't!" yelled Mary.

Colin's nurse was listening and she laughed, saying, "It's the best thing that could happen to the pampered thing, to have someone stand up to him that's as spoilt as himself!"

Later Colin had the most terrible tantrum. He screamed and yelled and sobbed, beat his pillow and thrashed around his bed.

"Stop it!" shouted Mary. "Or I'll scream too – and I can scream louder than you!"

"I can feel a lump on my back. I'm going to die!" gasped Colin.

"Nurse, show me his back," commanded Mary, sharply. She felt so cross and not a bit sorry for him.

Mary examined the thin, pale back. Finally, she declared, "There's nothing wrong with your back. If you ever say so again, I shall laugh!"

"His back is weak because he won't sit up," said the nurse.

Colin calmed down. Mary stayed with him and he went quiet and sleepy.

"Oh Mary," he whispered. "If only you could find the way into the secret garden . . . if I could only go there, I may live."

The day after this happened, Mary told Colin about the key. First of all, she talked to him about Dickon and the creatures of the moor who were his friends, like Jump the pony, and two squirrels called Nut and Shell. She told him that Dickon was going to visit him and bring the animals with him and then she said, "I've been in the garden . . . I couldn't tell you before. I had to be sure I could trust you."

The Doctor was astonished to see the change in his patient. Instead of lying in bed, he was sitting on a sofa and looking at gardening books with Mary.

"I'm going out soon," Colin said. "I need some fresh air. Dickon will push my carriage."

"You mustn't tire yourself," said the Doctor. "But you'll be safe with Dickon. He's as strong as a moor pony."

"He's the trustiest lad in Yorkshire," said Mary. She was learning to speak as the local people did.

What an amazing sight it was when Dickon brought the animals to show Colin! There was a lamb, a fox, two squirrels and a crow! Dickon placed the little lamb on Colin's lap and it nuzzled his velvet dressing gown.

COLIN SEES THE GARDEN!

They had to be sure that no-one knew where Colin was going. Colin told the gardeners not to be around each day at a certain time.

As he was wheeled through the gardens, Colin breathed deeply in the fresh, sweet-scented air and listened to all the sounds of the insects and birds.

Finally, they arrived at the secret garden. Dickon pushed the wheelchair quickly through the door, and Colin gasped with sheer delight and wonder. His face had a pink glow and he cried out, "I shall get well!"

Mary and Dickon did some work while Colin watched. He was delighted to be there and wanted to know about everything.

The afternoon came to an end.

"I'll come here every day," said Colin.

Suddenly, they were all startled to see an angry face peering over the wall!

"Ben!" cried Mary.

The cross old gardener shook his fist at them.

"The robin showed me the way," said Mary.

"Do you know who I am?" asked Colin.

Ben, still standing on a ladder, peered at Colin, then answered in a shaky voice, "Aye, I do. Th' cannot walk with th' crooked back and legs."

"Dickon, help me!" cried Colin, suddenly angry and defiant.

There was a fierce scramble and Colin threw all his rugs to the ground. Then, after a desperate struggle, he was standing upright on the grass.

"Look at me!" he yelled.

Mary gasped and went pale.

"He's as straight as I am," said Dickon.

Ben's eyes filled with tears as he murmured, "God bless ye."

Colin stared at Ben. "I'm your master when my father is away – and this is my garden!"

"Yes sir," answered Ben.

"It's magic!" said Dickon.

Colin stood proudly on his thin legs. "This was my mother's garden, wasn't it, Ben?"

"Aye. She loved it, an' she said to me, 'If I ever go away, take care of my roses.' So I used to come over the wall."

"I'm glad you did," said Colin. "You can keep our secret."

Colin grew to love his trips to the secret garden. "There's magic in there," he told Mary.

The months that followed seemed like magic too. All the buds began to unfurl and show every shade of blue, crimson and purple, and the scent of roses filled the air.

One day, Colin said to Mary, Dickon and Ben, "I want you all to listen carefully. When Mary found this garden, it looked dead. Then things began to happen and it came alive. When I grow up I intend to make great scientific discoveries and I shall start with this experiment. I call what happened magic. The magic in this garden made me stand up. Every day I'm going to say 'Magic is in me! Magic will make me as strong as Dickon!' And you must all help."

So they sat cross-legged in a circle and Colin said over and over again, "Magic is in me! Being alive is the magic! Being strong is the magic! Magic is in all of us!"

All this time, Colin's father was travelling in distant places. For ten years he had been heartbroken. But suddenly, he began to feel differently.

It was as if a shadow was lifting from him. "I feel almost alive," he thought.

When he arrived home, he asked where Colin was. Imagine his surprise when he was told, "In the garden."

What joy was Mr Craven's when he saw Colin!

"Father, I can hardly believe it myself!" said his son.

A little later, every servant stared in delight and wonder at Mr Craven walking across the lawn – and there, by his side, as straight and strong as any boy in Yorkshire, was Colin!

First published in this abridged version by
HarperCollins Publishers Ltd in 1988
First published in this paperback edition in 1993

Text © William Collins Sons & Company Ltd 1988
Illustrations © Alison Nicholson 1988